Running with Reed:

Be a Better Somebody

By Reed Kotalik

With Tammi Croteau Keen

Illustrated by Archangelo Crelencia

A Civin Media Relations project

2nd edition

ISBN-10: 1984051849

ISBN-13: 978-1984051844

Printed in the United States

Amazon Create Space

Project Managed by Todd Civin

www.civinmediarelations.com

Civin Media Relations

Dedication

This book is dedicated to my Mom, Dad, and four siblings - Grace, Rafe, Jarrett, and Noah.

And to those who have inspired me:

Grant Milton, Sawyer Khalaf, Logan Montgomery, and Lauren Walier.

- Reed Kotalik

When I run, I imagine that I am as fast as a lightning bolt shooting through the sky! I love to zoom around the track. It is so much fun!

Some people say I make running look easy, but that is not always the case. There are times that my legs turn in and that I feel weak.

Just before my fifth birthday, doctors said I had Cerebral Palsy. Those words sounded scary, but I learned that I could strengthen my muscles with exercise and training. I knew that I could face that challenge because I have big dreams.

Someday, I want to be in the Olympics. I have dreamed about winning gold in the distance races! I have imagined victory in the decathlon, too!

When I started training, I met Matt. He helped create my workouts. I practiced almost every day. I did leg lifts and lunges. I ran on a treadmill and walked up a climbing machine. I did speed drills and learned better balance.

Matt showed me how to warm up before races. I pushed myself so that I could build strength in my body. When my legs feel wobbly, I fight harder to get stronger. I don't mind because it helps me run fast like lightning.

Cerebral Palsy can affect people differently. Not only does it make my legs unsteady, but it also makes my vision become blurry.

It is part of me, but it is not who I am. After all my training, my mom asked if I wanted to sign up to play tee-ball. I told her I wanted to run in a road race instead. She thought that was a great idea.

My mom said there was a race planned for Thanksgiving morning. She registered me for the one mile. I was so excited to get to the start line. There were hundreds of people there, mostly grown-ups and bigger kids.

After the blare of the loud horn, the other runners' feet sounded like thunder on the ground. I focused on running fast like a lightning bolt. I saw my family cheering when I crossed the finish line.

I was excited to have won my first running trophy. We decided to celebrate. I was feeling hungry, so we went to get my very favorite breakfast - SPAGHETTI!!!!

As I ate with my family, I was daydreaming about running. I wanted to become even faster, like the speed of light. I couldn't wait to cross the finish line again!

I began training even harder and entered more races. I ran one that was five miles long! I was determined to become a better runner!

Matt watched over my running schedule because I didn't want to strain my muscles. I tried new track and field events. I loved throwing the turbo javelin and shotput. Jumping far into sand pits and over high bars was exciting too.

Of all the competitions, distance running was still my favorite. I won several national championships over the next two years.

One day a reporter from a magazine came to talk to me after a race. He said I inspired him and that he wanted to share my story. I spoke about my experiences and hoped that I could motivate others to follow their own dreams.

Later that day, I asked one of my brothers how I could do more to help our community. Rafe is really smart. He is only twelve years old, but he is almost an Eagle Scout. Rafe said, "You should make others feel like they can be somebody, too."

He challenged me to a short game of floor hockey. Afterwards, we sat down to make a list of ways to help other people. We came up with some great ideas!

On the top of my list was helping my little sister, Grace. She wanted to run a race. I helped her prepare and warmup. When we got to the start line, Grace looked really scared. I gave her a hug and told her, "You have got this!"

When I finished the race, I turned around and saw Grace in the distance behind me. She looked tired, so I ran back to her. She had her favorite blanket in her arms, so I wrapped it over her shoulders to help her feel strong like a superhero. When Grace crossed the finish line, we were both so happy. I guess we inspired each other.

"Helping other kids like me" was also on the list that I made with Rafe. I asked my mom if she knew anyone else with Cerebral Palsy. She told me about a little boy named Sawyer. Doctors told his parents that he may never be able to walk. I decided to do something to inspire Sawyer.

I tied photos of Sawyer on my running shoes. I sent him the medals from those races that I dedicated to him. Someday when he gets bigger, I want to be able to run with Sawyer. I hope I can motivate him to get stronger.

I had several big races coming up. My mom said that I could keep working on my list as we traveled. First, we flew to New York. I ran in a race to raise money to help others with Cerebral Palsy.

Then, I went to Nevada for a National Championship meet. I won six medals and qualified for Junior Olympics. My favorite part of the trip was what I did after competing each day. I delivered school supplies and books for homeless children.

After my summer meets, I took time off from training. I wanted to work on my list. "Spending time with family and friends" was important to me.

My friend, Max, invited me to swim in his pool. I told him that I couldn't swim. Max said that he could help me. I was excited to learn water skills. It felt great to try something new with my friend.

During my break from training, some of my other friends invited me to play flag football. Running in touchdowns made me feel even stronger, just in a different way.

I shared my list with Aidan, Anderson, Ashton, and Ehren! We challenged each other to do 21 kind acts in ONE day and our moms agreed to help with our BIG plan. We tackled the list together. We delivered cookies to firefighters, gave board games to senior citizens, gathered food for a pantry, cleaned a pond, and put together many care packages for others. I loved helping with my friends.

Over the past few years since I was diagnosed with Cerebral Palsy, I have learned so much.

I have realized that the best part about being an athlete isn't the medals or trophies. It is challenging myself to be better and stronger. The best part of helping others is sharing my hope that I will inspire them to do the same.

I have learned that, above all else, we can all be a better somebody TOGETHER.

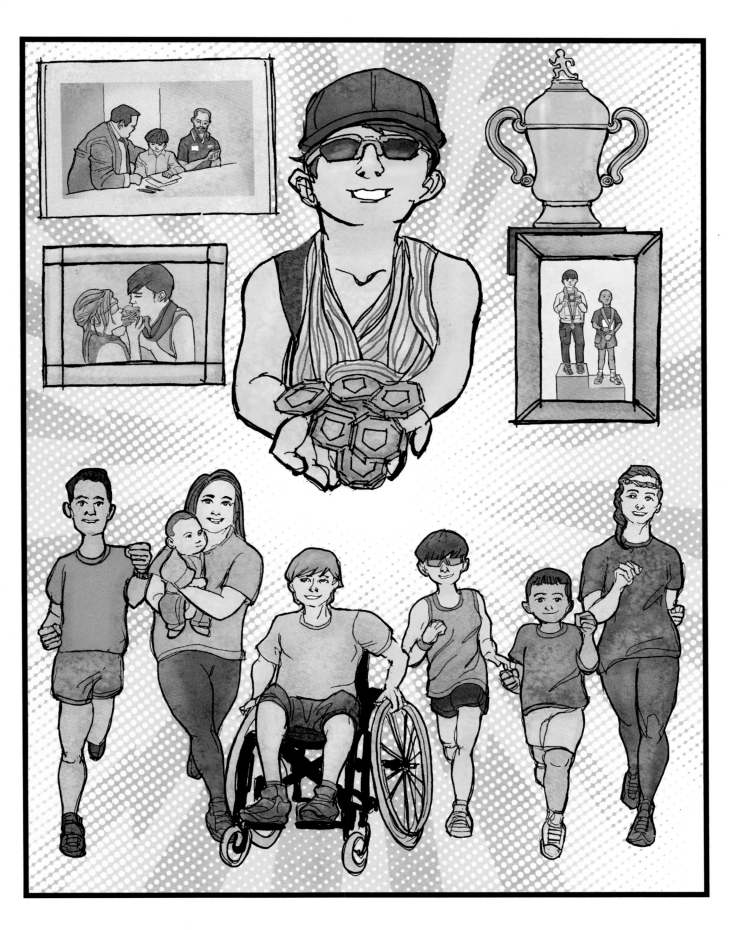

I know there is a chance that my legs won't let me run like lightning forever, but I am going to give it my best for as long as I can.

My life has been pretty awesome so far, but I'm just getting started. It doesn't matter whether my future holds more National Championships, flag football games, or even a hockey season or two. What matters most is that I know I am somebody and that I want to inspire others!

Who knows?

Maybe Rafe and I will become inventors and make seeds that grow hamburgers. Or maybe, Grace and I will open a shop and sell magical ice cream cones. Or maybe, Sawyer and I will own a professional hockey team. Or maybe, Max and I will design the coolest waterslide in the country.

Or maybe, my football friends and I will set a world record for the number of kind acts that can be done in one day.

While there is so much I can do in the future, I will keep at the top of my list to be the best brother, a great friend, and to always be a better somebody.

I know that I am young, but I can make a difference and so can you! Don't be scared to try. Start with something small to brighten someone's day. Always remember, you have got this! Follow you heart, dream big, and help others along the way!

"You Have Come a Long Way"

About Reed Kotalik

By his parents, Dawn and John Kotalik

No matter whether Reed is running on an oval, trail, or road, with each step we never take for granted what he has overcome these past eight years. It is nothing short of a miracle that Reed can take part in the sport that he loves. Reed was born with laryngomalacia. He labored to breathe as a baby. After extensive testing, doctors determined that he had no cartilage in his throat. Initially, medical professionals suggested that he would "outgrow" the condition, but that wasn't the case. With any little sickness, the "floppy" throat tissue would swell and inhibit his breathing. After a lengthy hospitalization following his first birthday, surgeons intervened and repaired his throat. Feeding and other therapy followed.

Once he got past those hurdles, neurological and muscular deficiencies became more noticeable as he was learning to walk. Reed would wake multiple times through the night and cry out, but not recognize us when we rushed to aid him. Doctors suspected the episodes were seizures and more studies followed as we searched for answers.

Near Thanksgiving of 2014, the neurologist diagnosed Reed with Cerebral Palsy. Surgery was suggested along with seizure medication. Instead of rushing into this new path for our little boy with the biggest blue eyes and the sweetest smile, we decided to wait until after the holidays to proceed with the treatment plan.

During those weeks, we spent time exploring other treatment possibilities and Reed shared his thoughts. For Reed, the diagnosis was life changing but not in the way that most would expect. From that point, we followed his lead and remain in awe as to where it has taken us. His path was one that required a lot of persistence and significant rehabilitation to strengthen and condition muscles. There have been challenges, including cardiac episodes and weakness after illness, but he never veers from his path.

Since the start of 2015, Reed has stepped up to 33 national podiums across the country. He has won 9 national championships in running and field events. In the spring of 2016, he partnered with CHI St. Luke's Health and Rad Rabbit. Since then, Reed's running has taken on added meaning - to bring awareness to Cerebral Palsy, CASA for foster kids, Batten Disease, Head for the Cure, and Juvenile Diabetes. Reed was named the national ambassador for the Make Lemon Aide for Cerebral Palsy Foundation. In February of 2017, AAU Track and Field named Reed as its national spotlight athlete. In August 2017, Reed challenged friends to join him to do 21 Random Acts of Kindness in one day to honor friend Grant Milton. Reed makes public appearances to benefit literacy causes, has hosted drives to gather books for hospitalized children, and provided school supplies and toys for those in foster care. When he isn't running, Reed loves fishing, exploring the American backcountry by train, painting, and his favorite superhero is Flash. Thanks for sharing in the journey with us and for being part of TEAM REED!

Acknowledgements

Special thanks to all those who have been a source of
encouragement and guidance over the past couple of years.
It is in your support that I have found the greatest of super powers.

To CHI St. Luke's Health for providing me with the best sports medicine
resources, performance "home," and trainers -
especially Mr. Rashard, Mrs. Amy, Mr. Andy, and Mr. Matt.

To Monica DeVreese, Jill Deering, and the rest of my rabbit family for
allowing me to help represent the future of this sport with
runinrabbit.com.

To Chris Bilbrew, Dan Green, Eric Henry, Brock Moreaux, Jarrett LeBlanc,
Sam McClellan, Will Stewart, Lindsay Schwartz, Barbara Nwaba, and
Tom Fitzsimons for being the best running and multi-event mentors!

To Lauren Walier and Sherry Walier for honoring me as the ambassador
for their national non-profit, Make Lemon Aide for Cerebral Palsy.

To my beloved, former teachers and Miss Nicolette Hardwicke at Paddington British Private School for providing the best foundation for my education and for building my confidence through an amazing fine arts curriculum.

To Mrs. Brown, Mrs. McCormick, Mrs. Silveira, and the rest of the staff at David for your efforts to develop my reading skills, creative writing, and overall encouragement to be the best student that I can be.

To Mrs. Tammi Croteau Keen, Civin Media Relations, and Mr. Archangelo Crelencia for giving me this opportunity to write this book and share my story.

To Grace for being my biggest cheerleader, to Rafe for being my guide, to Jarrett for being my "shadow" during races, to Noah for helping with my gear, and to my parents for showing their unwavering support and never-ending love every day.

And to DeDe, Pop, Grandma, Grandpa, for loving me and always reminding me that "it's no hill for a climber."

- Reed Kotalik

About Civin Media Relations

We hear your voice. Let's tell your story.

Civin Media Relations believes that words can change the world. They offer a full range of creative and technical services to help you share your story. For more information on CMR, and to view other available titles, connect with us on social media or visit civinmediarelations.com.

CMR founder Todd Civin with his wife, Katie, and athlete Rick Hoyt

---

Illustrator Archangelo Crelencia, a former US Air Force graphics specialist, draws his inspiration from sci-fi, animation, music, and comic books. He holds a BFA degree in Visual Communications and resides in Chicago, where he works as an art director/storyboard artist in the advertising industry. To see more of Angelo's work, follow him on social media @TheArchangelo, or visit his website, TheArchangelo.com.

Co-Author Tammi Croteau Keen enjoys redefining the fairy tale in her children's books. She is a Public Affairs Officer in the Army National Guard and a full-time government analyst. In her spare time, Tammi performs as an oboist with the Mansfield Wind Symphony. She holds degrees in Music, English/Creative Writing, and Emergency Management. To view more of Tammi's work, visit tammicroteaukeen.com or connect with her on social media.